Hilbre

Islands in the Dee Estuary

Margaret Sixsmith

To those who wish to preserve and protect the islands and enjoy the peace
and solitude that can be found there

THE DEE ESTUARY IS A DANGEROUS PLACE.
THE TIDE CAN RETURN VERY QUICKLY.
VISITORS TO HILBRE MUST TAKE RESPONSIBILITY FOR THEIR OWN SAFETY AND BE
ADEQUATELY PREPARED FOR THEIR VISIT.
SAFE CROSSING TIMES ARE ALWAYS DISPLAYED AT DEE LANE SLIPWAY.

First Published 2006 by Countyvise Limited, 14 Appin Road, Birkenhead,
Wirral CH41 9HH.

Copyright © 2006 Margaret Sixsmith

The right of Margaret Sixsmith to be identified as the author of this work has been
asserted by her in accordance with the Copyright, Design and Patents Act 1988.

British Library Cataloguing in Publication Data.
A catalogue record for this book is available from the British Library.

Please note: From 1st January 2007 ISBNs will contain 13 numbers; these numbers
will be the same as the present number printed below the barcode (ie. starting 978).
Countyvise is showing both existing (10 digit) and future (13 digit) ISBNs on the
Title page verso. Please continue to use the 10 figure number until 31st December
2006.

ISBN 1 901231 64 X   ISBN 978 1 901231 64 9

Contents

Barnacles

Introduction

The three Hilbre islands, Little Eye, Middle Eye and Hilbre are a unique feature of the Wirral landscape. Situated in the mouth of the Dee estuary one mile out from the Wirral mainland, they are cut off by the tide twice a day. Now owned by Wirral Metropolitan Borough Council (WMBC), they are managed as a Local Nature Reserve with a resident Ranger and are an important part of the Dee Estuary grade 1 Site of Special Scientific Interest (SSSI), Ramsar site (a wetland of international importance), SPA (Special Protection Area), SAC (Special Area of Conservation) and RIGS (Regionally Important Geological and Geomorphological Site).

The aim of this book is to give a brief look at the history and to act as a guide to the visible natural history of the islands.

Route

Access to the Hilbre islands is by walking across the two miles of estuary from West Kirby at low tide.

West Kirby is on the North West of the Wirral peninsula. From Liverpool take the M53 from the Wallasey tunnel, leave at junction 2 and follow the A5027, B5139 and A540 to West Kirby. From Chester follow the A540 to West Kirby. Once in West Kirby follow the brown marine lake signs to Dee Lane.

Car parking is available free along the one-way South Parade and in the nearby car park (fee).

There is a train station and local buses stop in West Kirby.

Toilets are at Dee Lane open 10am-6pm.

Safe crossing times are always displayed at Dee Lane slipway.

Allow at least an hour for the crossing but be aware that strong winds may bring the tide in early or suddenly. Stout footwear is recommended as the rocks are sharp and slippery and there are weever fish submerged in the low tide channels in the estuary.

The route begins from the slipway at Dee Lane next to the Marine Lake and continues across the estuary towards Little Eye. Turn right at Little Eye and walk past Middle Eye keeping the island on the left and take the rough track over the rocks to the south end

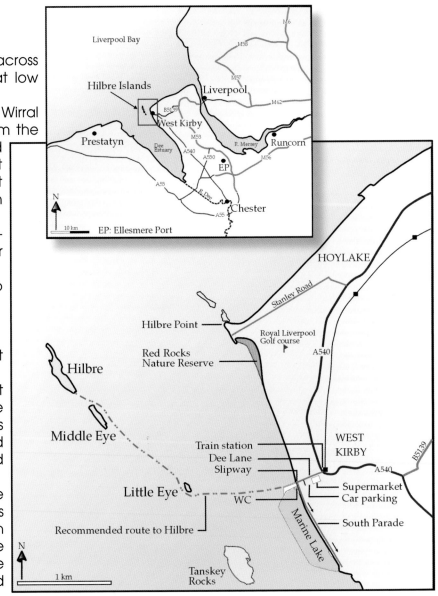

of Hilbre. Alternatively there is a well-marked path across Middle Eye. Once on the main island the paths are very well marked.

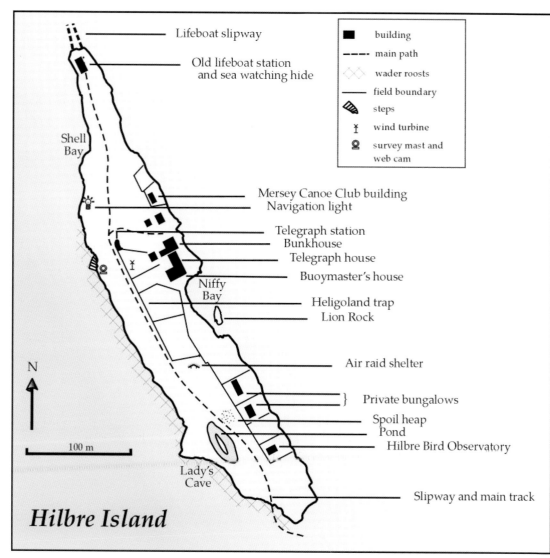

Lifeboat slipway

Old lifeboat station and sea watching hide

Shell Bay

building

----- main path

wader roosts

field boundary

steps

wind turbine

survey mast and web cam

Mersey Canoe Club building
Navigation light

Telegraph station
Bunkhouse
Telegraph house
Buoymaster's house

Niffy Bay

Heligoland trap
Lion Rock

N

Air raid shelter

} Private bungalows

Spoil heap
Pond
Hilbre Bird Observatory

100 m

Lady's Cave

Slipway and main track

Hilbre Island

There are no facilities whatsoever on Hilbre so adequate preparations for a high tide visit are needed. Waterproofs, extra clothing, hot drink and food are all required. To stay the 5 hours over high tide leave West Kirby at least 3 hours before high tide. (3½ hours on tides above 9.5m). A permit is required for groups of 6 or more people and these are available from: The Visitor Centre, Wirral Country Park, Station Road, Thurstaston, Wirral CH61 0HN,
Tel: 0151 648 4371/3884.
The Visitor Centre is open daily from 10am-5pm.
On a low tide visit, allow 3 hours to return from Hilbre before high tide.

DO NOT ATTEMPT TO CROSS FROM RED ROCKS OR DIRECTLY FROM WEST KIRBY.

Geology

Lion Rock

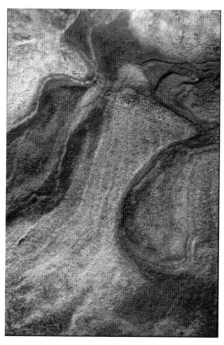

Sandstone patterns

The Hilbre islands are formed from a ridge of Bunter Sandstone, a sedimentary rock succession deposited during the Triassic period (180million to 225million years ago). This ridge also extends south towards Caldy, being visible at low tide at Tanskey rocks. Many interesting features indicating the origin of the rocks of the Hilbre islands can be found by examining the cliff faces and rock formations on the islands. Cross-bedding, formed from the migration of ancient sand dunes, and pebble beds laid down in ancient river courses, have given geologists clues as to how rocks of the Triassic period were formed. The footprints from Chirotherium dinosaurs that have been found on the island also indicate the types of animal in this period.

The islands originally formed part of the mainland and probably became tidal during the time of fluctuating sea levels in the Mesolithic period about 8,000 years ago.

What is left of the islands today is the result of several thousand years of erosion by the sea. Many interesting features caused by this sea erosion can be seen, including cliffs, sea caves, stacks, arches and wave cut platforms.

Fault in sandstone

Sea caves form when the erosive power of waves exploits a weakness towards the base of a cliff face. This could be a fault in the rock or where a rock-boring animal has created a small hole for the waves to exploit. Continued erosion of the caves leads to the formation of blowholes and sea arches. When the roof of a sea arch collapses this leaves a vertical pillar of rock called a sea stack. Over time, these sea stacks can eventually be weathered away.

Dinosaur footprints

Sea arches can be found on the south end of Middle Eye and the arch on the east side of Hilbre has already been repaired with concrete and stones to prevent the narrow neck collapsing.

Cross-bedding on Middle Eye

History

Lady's Cave legends.
There are many folk stories relating to the naming of Lady's Cave.

Many are based around the story of a young lady sailing to Wales for an arranged marriage against her will. She threw herself overboard and was washed up into the cave where she told her story to one of the monks on the island and died in his arms.

Another story relates to a ship's figurehead being found in the cave and so giving the cave its name.

Old lifeboat station

Many clues have been found on the islands to help unravel Hilbre's past.

Shell middens and flints left by hunter-gatherers from the Mesolithic period have been found on Little Eye and Hilbre.

Neolithic remains found include flints and an axe head. Other finds include a Bronze Age burial urn, axe head, burnt stone mound, kitchen middens, ancient land boundaries and buried land surfaces on Middle Eye. Roman pottery has been found on Hilbre, suggesting Roman occupation, but no structural evidence of this has ever been unearthed. Some of the finds from the islands are kept at the Grosvenor Museum, Chester and at Liverpool Museum.

An Anglo-Norse crosshead dated about 1000 AD and a carved grave slab dated about 1100 AD have also been found on Hilbre. These stones are kept at the Grosvenor Museum, Chester and at the Charles Dawson Museum at St Bridget's Church, West Kirby.

Some of Hilbre's more recent history, as written in Victorian times, is a little unclear. Recent historical research has uncovered documents that were clearly not available to the Victorian historians. These documents are helping to unravel the truth behind the stories and legends that the Victorians believed.

Old tide gauge

Hilbre was once known as Hildeburgheye and the Victorians believed that the name was from a Saint Hildeburgh. However, to date, no records have been found showing a Saint Hildeburgh in the British Isles. The name may well have been in honour of a local Saxon lady.

The earliest known written records come from the 11th century when the French abbot of the Abbey at St Evroult in Normandy asked William 1st of England for funds to help his monastery through a bad time. This help was a package of presents, including churches and villages from all over midland Britain. The rent and taxes from the villages would provide welcome funds to help the monastery. In 1081 this included the estate of West Kirby, Hilbre and the two chapels, one on Hilbre and the other in the town, probably St Bridget's. Later, Hilbre and West Kirby were probably found to be too far away to be considered a useful investment and St Evroult transferred this estate to Chester Abbey. However, Basingwerk Abbey in Flintshire also claimed the estate and there were furious battles for possession of West Kirby and Hilbre in the Chester courts. Eventually this was settled and Hilbre became the property of Chester Abbey and West Kirby became the property of Basingwerk Abbey.

From this time it is known that two monks from Chester Abbey and their servants were living on the island, the chapel there being dedicated to St Mary the blessed Virgin. The monks collected taxes for the Abbey and also ran two boats. One was a small fishing boat and the other a larger craft, possibly used for inshore trading or fishing for herring in Liverpool Bay.

North cone & old navigation light

Photo courtesy of Val McFarland

The Victorians believed that there were pilgrimages to the chapel on Hilbre but recent research has thrown doubt on this. No written documentation of papal permission has been found to date for Hilbre to hold a pilgrimage. It is more likely that the so-called pilgrimage was a visit by the local people to an annual service held at the chapel on Hilbre on the 15th August. Over the years this annual visit may have been confused with the documented pilgrimage to St Winifrede at Holywell in nearby Flintshire. Around this time, there are also stories of a light in the chapel on Hilbre which the Victorians believed to be a mariners beacon. Once the monks had left the island after the dissolution of the abbeys this light was no longer mentioned and is more likely to have been a votive lamp given to the Hilbre chapel in memory of somebody's deceased relative.

When Chester Abbey was disbanded in 1540, the monks were recalled from the island. In anticipation of this the abbot let out Hilbre as a tenancy to a local squire in 1538. The lease soon passed to the Stanley family of Hooton, important army commanders in the Royal campaigns in Ireland. Hilbre then became a boarding point for soldiers and supplies. For the next 150 years, small locally owned ships, such as those which had traded with Dublin for centuries, now carried thousands of troops from many Dee and Wirral harbours.

A footing for the northern perch

The monks' house, rebuilt several times, continued to be accommodation for the tenants but eventually, along with the chapel, disappeared completely. The present stone buildings, rebuilt in Victorian times, probably occupy the site of this house.

When the Irish campaigns ended in 1690, Hilbre's importance as an embarkation point for troops declined. In 1692 there was a salt boiling business on the main island. A rock cut cistern on the shore just below the eastern cliffs is all that remains from this enterprise. In 1755 there were plans to establish an oyster fishery around the islands but this was fiercely opposed by local people and traders and never went ahead. A public house, possibly called The Seagull Inn, was licensed on Hilbre between 1793 and 1826. The landlord, Joseph Hickson, was widely believed to be a successful smuggler, as he was never caught!

Hilbre was very important for shipping throughout past centuries; its harbour, along with that of Liverpool, was under the supervision of the chief port at that time, which was Chester.

The approaches to the Rivers Dee and Mersey are very dangerous especially to the sailing ships around at this time and many were lost in the local waters. This meant that the sailing guides on Hilbre were very important. The earliest guides were probably tall wooden masts or perches, put up in the early eighteenth century at the north and south ends of Hilbre. The footings for the northern perch were deep rectangles cut in the bare rock. These are still visible and at one time mistakenly believed to be monks' graves. The perches were demolished and replaced by shore marks, the ruined concrete and stone base of one is still visible on Little Eye.

In 1827 the Trustees of the Liverpool Docks, an organisation of Liverpool councillors and businessmen, obtained the lease of the islands from Chester Cathedral (as Chester Abbey had now become). They built a telegraph signalling station on the main island as part of the Welsh chain of semaphore stations. This linked Anglesey with the Liverpool Docks Office on the Mersey waterfront and was operated by telegraph keepers. When Atlantic merchant ships were sighted off Wales, the message of their safe return could be signalled in

Remains of the old shore mark on Little Eye

daylight by coded semaphore messages, reaching Liverpool within a few minutes. The record is believed to be 23 seconds but in poor weather and at night, it was unusable. The nearest of the 12 stations to Hilbre was above Prestatyn, and is now a private house.

The first temporary telegraph semaphore building on Hilbre was erected in 1827. The site of this is the flat patch of ground that can be seen to the north of its replacement, the present telegraph station. This was built in 1841 along with a house for the telegraph keeper.

At first the telegraph station was flat-roofed, but it was converted to a cable telegraph system about 20 years later and the pitched slate roof was added. A weather vane in the form of an arrow stood on the roof and worked a pointer inside the ceiling of the building. This meant that the keeper on duty could read the wind direction without leaving his post. Telescopes were mounted in the five movable brass

Mersey Canoe Club clubhouse

gimbals in the bay window. Watch was kept in all the daylight hours, monitoring stationary vessels such as the lightship in Liverpool Bay, as well as Liverpool's marine traffic.

During this time, the telegraph keepers kept a horse or pony for transport, cows, pigs and poultry for their own use and sheep to keep the grass short. Hilbre and Middle Eye were also divided into fields, the faint boundaries of which can still be seen on Middle Eye. Hay was cut in the paddocks, and corn was grown on the southern end of Hilbre. Vegetables were grown in the garden.

In 1849 the lifeboat station and slipway were built as an annexe to the lifeboat station at Hoylake for use at low water. However, this became redundant when a tractor was obtained in 1938 to pull Hoylake's lifeboat to the water's edge at all states of the tide. (The slipway was badly damaged by storms in 2000, but repairs are planned soon.)

Trinity House, the organisation set up to help marine navigation, leased part of the island from the Dock Trustees. They built the Buoymaster's house and associated workshops in 1850 and this enabled them to maintain a depot for cleaning and repairing buoys in the Dee and North Wales channels. Their large workshop still stands and the complement of stables, barns, boathouse, pigsties and outdoor conveniences are still largely intact.

Around 1852-3 a tide gauge was built in a deep channel alongside the slipway to be able to predict the times and heights of the tides. This is still in use today but has now been computerised. The Trustees changed their name to the Mersey Docks and Harbour Board and in 1856 bought Hilbre from Chester Cathedral.

The Mersey Docks and Harbour Board leased the property that had been built by Trinity House to private individuals after the buoy store was discontinued in 1876. Hilbre was now becoming popular for yachts and sailing boats. The Mersey Canoe Club was formed and granted permission to build a clubhouse in 1897. Other holiday bungalows were erected in 1897, 1905, 1908 and 1928.

As Hilbre began to become popular for day-trippers, some of them behaving very badly, the Dock Board and tenants became increasingly concerned and attempts to prevent public access were made. Iron railings and gates were erected around Middle Eye and Hilbre in 1911 and a system of issuing tickets, obtained in advance, was tried. Even a policeman was employed on Sundays to try and enforce regulations. Naturally there was public outcry to all these restrictions, but the ticket system of control was generally agreed to be in the best interest of all parties. This ticket system continued with slight alterations right up to the present day and now a permit is only required for parties of more than six people.

In 1927 a flashing light signal was established for marine navigation. Trinity House took responsibility for this in 1973 when it was rebuilt and automated. It was converted from acetylene gas to solar power in 1995.

During the First World War the Army occupied Hilbre islands. Only the tenants and telegraph keepers were allowed on the islands and were challenged by the soldiers when they arrived. Once their identity was established, they were allowed to go free. The soldiers were on the lookout for possible spies and any suspicious characters that were caught were escorted to the Colonel in nearby Birkenhead to be dealt with appropriately.

Hilbre Bird Observatory

During the Second World War, the RAF devised an elaborate nationwide decoy system known as the Starfish decoy system to deceive enemy aircraft away from major targets. The decoy system on the Hilbre islands was designed so that an electric current would be sent through cables from Hilbre and ignite materials such as oil barrels on Middle Eye. This would then imitate the burning Mersey docklands, and so deceive the second wave of enemy aircraft to drop their bombs there instead of hitting Birkenhead and Liverpool. Despite a chain of such decoys throughout Wirral, the system was never used. The mound of earth next to the main track on Hilbre hid the system's generator as well as serving as an air raid shelter and the cables are still visible in a concrete block at the south end of the island.

In 1945, modern navigation equipment meant that Hilbre was redundant as a signal station, and the Mersey Docks and Harbour Board sold the three islands as a nature reserve to the Hoylake Urban District Council. Various safeguards were put in place to protect the islands from undesirable development. The present owners, WMBC, maintain the islands as a public open space and nature reserve.

In 1954 the islands were first given SSSI (Site of Special Scientific Interest) status and in 1983 they were declared a Local Nature Reserve. They have since become part of the Dee Estuary Ramsar site. In 1985 the post of Custodian was changed to Coastal Ranger with responsibility for the Hilbre islands and the Dee estuary. The ranger lives in the telegraph keeper's house.

The main developments on Hilbre after the Second World War have been by local naturalists. There is now a well-established bird observatory based in the building at the southern end of Hilbre. The members of the observatory converted the interior of the lifeboat station into a sea watching hide for ornithologists.

A storm cone was used from early in the 20th century to warn shipping of imminent northerly or southerly gales. This was of

Plaque, Telegraph keeper's house

particular interest to ornithologists. Northerly gales, particularly in autumn, could result in sightings of rare seabirds that had been blown off course. Also in the 20th century Hilbre was fitted with a survey mast so that the Dee sandbanks and channels could be drawn on sailing charts. This mast has now been replaced and fitted with radar, a weather station and web camera (web site: www.wirralcam.com or www.wirral.gov.uk)

The paddock behind the Ranger's house is in such an exposed position that the paint industry have used it in the past to test their paint products. A rack filled with painted pieces of metal was erected and the resulting weathering of the colour and type of paint was monitored. This was removed once the industry found other ways of testing their products.

In 2001 The Friends of Hilbre was formed joining other voluntary groups working on Hilbre under the direction of the Coastal Ranger and WMBC. They are also involved in raising funds to help with the conservation of the islands and their buildings. In 2003 they restored the telegraph station.
Web site: www.hilbreisland.org.uk

Permission was given in late 2004 for the Buoymaster's house to be converted into a community research and study centre and the lifeboat slipway to be repaired. This will go ahead once the necessary funding has been found.

In early spring 2005 a small wind turbine was erected to supply the Ranger's house and the radar station with electricity.

Present day Hilbre

The Islands

Islands in the Dee Estuary

Sunset over Little Eye

Little Eye is the first island to be reached on the route to Hilbre. Sea erosion has not left very much of this island but it is still an important high tide roost during the winter months mainly for oystercatchers and gulls. However, if they are disturbed they do tend to favour Middle Eye as their safe haven over the high tide.

From Little Eye the recommended route turns right following the ridge of sandstone towards the second island, Middle Eye. On approaching Middle Eye, sea stacks and arches are visible. There are some very strange looking eroded sandstone rocks around the island and if taken out of context they could be mountain ranges from elsewhere in the world. All over the main two islands the eroded rocks can fire the imagination.

The top path over Middle Eye can give some remarkable views of the surrounding land. The Great Orme in North Wales is easily visible. On an exceptionally clear day the mountains of Snowdonia, southern Lake District and western Pennines can easily be seen.

The eerie sound of the Atlantic grey seals hauled out on Hoyle Bank can be heard from here. In the summer the Ranger sometimes sets up a telescope so that visitors may easily see the seals.

Little Eye

Eroded rocks

On reaching Hilbre Island the main path can be followed winding up the west side of the island. This west side takes the brunt of the high tides especially with a northwest gale blowing. The sandstone here has been eroded into exceptionally interesting formations. There are parts where it looks as if the sea spray has bleached the red sandstone yellow.

Walking up the main path the first building on the right is the Hilbre Bird Observatory. WMBC leases the next bungalows. On the left can be seen the man made pond believed to have been there since at least 1881. The small mound on the right is the spoil heap

Bluebells

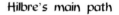

Hilbre's main path

from when the pond was excavated. The old air raid shelter can be seen a little further up on the right hand side.

Behind the fence is one of the Heligoland bird traps that the bird ringers use and the last building next to the path is the telegraph station, refurbished by the Friends of Hilbre in 2003 as an interpretation centre. Looking right from the telegraph station, Telegraph house, outbuildings and the recently erected wind turbine are visible. The Mersey Canoe Club owns the green building to the left of Telegraph house.

Opposite the telegraph station is the survey mast and web cam and a little further along is the navigation light maintained by Trinity House. Continuing along the path over the two stone bridges the site of the lifeboat station can be reached. Members of the bird observatory have converted part of the old lifeboat station into a hide, as this is the best vantage point for sea watching. Situated in the bricked off part at the end of the deep channel is the tide gauge.

Sea stack, Middle Eye

Nature
The Dee Estuary

Dee Estuary

Snowstorm approaching Little Eye

The Hilbre islands are situated in the Dee estuary and this estuary is so rich in invertebrates that tens of thousands of wading birds spend the winter there. It is an invaluable source of food for them when they return from their northern breeding grounds from August onwards. Some will use the estuary to rest, moult and gather their strength ready for the rest of the journey to their over-wintering grounds but many will stay on the estuary for the winter.

There are many signs of the abundant life beneath the surface of the estuary. The invertebrates will burrow to different depths in the mud and sand

Wader footprints and lugworm casts

Waders at the water's edge

Sand patterns

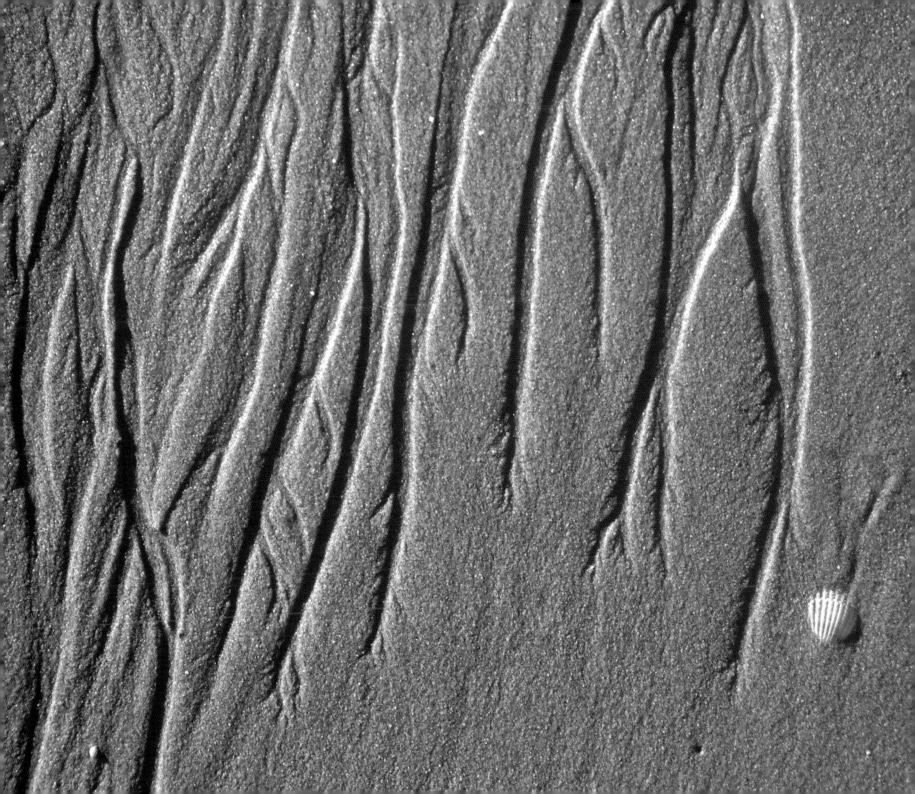

once the tide recedes. Many leave telltale signs of their presence. Living cockles eject small jets of water when they are disturbed and the lugworms leave behind large worm casts as they burrow into the sand. All marine life has to find a refuge when the tide is out and amongst the retreating running water many small animals can be found. Shrimps, prawns and small flatfish will all look for a pool to hide in until the tide returns and shore crabs will bury themselves into the wet sand. Lesser weever fish may also be lying just under the sand and their poisonous spines will be the only part seen protruding. These will inflict a very painful wound if trodden on by a bare foot.

The wading birds will follow the tide out looking for their favourite food. To avoid competition each species of wading bird has a different length beak. Curlews, with their long beaks, can easily reach the lugworms buried up to 30cm below the surface, and the abundant ragworms are food for many of the other waders. Oystercatchers are very fond of cockles and mussels. Redshank and shelduck are particularly fond of the tiny black hydrobia snails that can be seen scattered over the surface just after high tide.

Incoming tide

Shore crab

Shells & seaweed

Mermaid's purse & common whelk egg cases

Sand gaper shell

Many of the empty shells from these animals are found on the surface of the sand, the cockles and mussels being the most conspicuous. Others that can be found here include the pink and white shells of *Macoma* (nicknamed babies toenails), razor and oyster shells. The tide will bring in shells from deep water and leave them stranded on the sandy shore. These can include scallops, necklace shells and large whorled whelks. Empty sand gaper shells can sometimes be found in great numbers on the seaward side between Little and Middle Eye.

Other interesting remains can be found on the sand after the tide has receded. The common whelk (a large sea snail) deposits its sponge like egg masses into the sea and these are often washed up along the strand line. Fragile pieces of sea potato (a burrowing urchin) are sometimes found along with mermaids' purses, which are the empty egg cases of various rays, skates and dogfish.

Curlew

Lugworm casts

As the tide returns, all the wading birds will continue to feed at the water's edge, but will look for a safe place to roost over high tide. The islands themselves are extremely important roost sites along with the more inaccessible areas along the mainland shoreline.

Assorted shells on the beach at Shell Bay

Nature
The Rocky Shores

Sabellaria reef

Seaweeds

The rocky shores around the two larger islands provide a large intertidal surface area where many varieties of seaweed have colonised the different microhabitats provided by the eroding rocks.

The seaweeds are zoned according to their tolerance of dehydration between tides and the amount of exposure to waves. Those that live in the rock pools are never found on open rock and are amongst the prettiest of the seaweeds that can be seen.

All the seaweeds provide grazing and shelter for many crustaceans, molluscs and other small animals, which in turn provide food for larger marine mammals and birds.

There are plenty of barnacles and mussels, which are food for the dog whelks.

Periwinkles

Beadlet anemone

Limpets, barnacles and periwinkles

These snails deposit large numbers of yellow flask-shaped egg capsules into rock crevices.

Three species of winkles are found on the rocky shores. The grey rough periwinkle graze on micro-organisms and detritus. The smooth black or coloured flat periwinkle is found on the lower shore feeding on serrated wrack. The edible periwinkle is found all over the middle and lower shore amongst the seaweed.

On walking around the west side of Middle Eye towards the main island, the extensive colony of the honeycomb worm, *Sabellaria alveolata* can be seen. This is a soft coral-like reef as the tube that the worm inhabits is made from coarse cemented sand or shell grains. The honeycomb-like outcrops of the reef extend right around the islands starting on

Dog whelk eggs

Sandy Sabellaria reef

the west side of Middle Eye and continuing around Hilbre to the east side. The reef is still spreading and small amounts are present on the breakwaters of the North Wirral shore. As the worm's tubes are soft, the reef is fragile and visitors are asked not to trample on it.

It is interesting to see that the reef is made of mostly sand on the seaward side of Middle Eye, yet at Shell Bay, some of the reef is constructed with tiny shell grains.

As the individual reefs are made from sand or tiny shell grains, they tend to come and go but new colonies are formed regularly. Sometimes the worms will settle into older colonies thereby helping the reef itself outlast the individual worm. Individual worms usually live for between two and five years with spawning occurring in July.

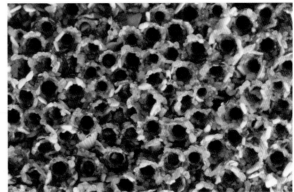

Shell Sabellaria reef

The larvae spend between six weeks and six months as plankton.

The sea slater, an unusual two-tailed member of the woodlouse family, can be found on the walls and in the caves at Shell Bay.

Minute grey thrips float in patches on the surface of the rock pools on the upper shoreline.

Sea anemones, especially beadlet anemones, occur further down the shore and these are eaten by sea slugs. The beautiful white or orange plumose anemones can only be found at the lowest ebb tides right on the north end of Hilbre Island itself.

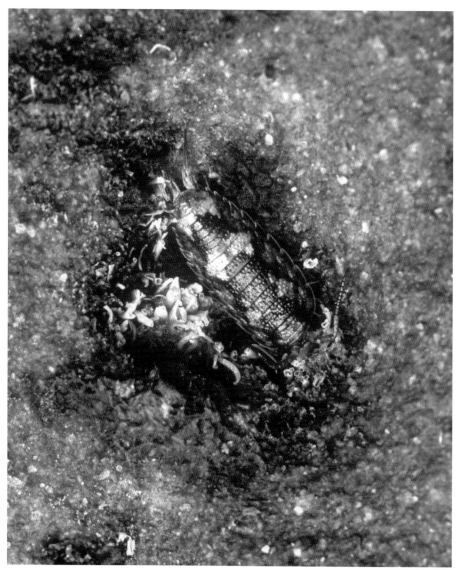

Channelled wrack

Sea slater

Nature

Birds

Oystercatchers on Little Eye

Waders landing on Hilbre

Hilbre's geographical location makes the islands a very important stop over point for many types of migratory bird in the spring and autumn. A few birds breed on the islands and these, along with the surrounding sands, are a productive place for many waders to spend the winter.

In post war years, a group of keen birdwatchers meeting on the islands realised that Hilbre would be a good place to study birds, especially the migratory ones. In 1957 the Hilbre Bird Observatory (HiBO) was established with the aim of watching, studying and ringing birds on and around the islands.

Two of the founder members, John Gittins and Professor John Craggs, became long-standing members and set up the foundations of the Hilbre Bird Observatory. The importance of their work was soon realised by the local Council and in 1962 they were provided with a cabin sited at the north end of the island. As the membership grew the Observatory was offered the most southerly bungalow on the Island. This provided a lot more space than the original cabin and is where the Hilbre Bird Observatory is presently situated.

Various traps are used to catch the birds and these include mist nets, cage and Heligoland traps. One of the Heligoland traps can be seen from the main path behind the fence when approaching the north end of the island.

The comprehensive records of the birds that have been trapped and ringed on the island have provided invaluable information on bird migration throughout Northern Europe and beyond.
It has been shown from these records that over-wintering knot and turnstone come mainly from Northern Canada and Greenland and the redshank from Iceland and the UK. Dunlin breed in northern Scandinavia, Iceland and Greenland and over-wintering sanderling breed mainly in the USSR. Oystercatcher breed in Scotland, Scandinavia, Iceland and the Faeroes. The records indicate the purple sandpipers over-wintering on Hilbre come from the Greenland/Canada area.

Roosting knot on Little Eye

Birdwatching is good all year on Hilbre, with each season having its specialities. Staying over a high tide on Hilbre during the autumn and winter months provides a chance of seeing rarities out to sea as well as the visiting over-wintering flocks of waders.

Birds in autumn and winter

The migratory birds use the islands as a stop off point on passage from their northerly breeding grounds to their over-wintering grounds further south. Some use the islands as a winter refuge and stay for the whole of the winter.

Purple sandpiper is a very regular winter visitor and will begin to return in the middle of October. In a good year by the end of November the flock can be as many as 50 birds. They will stay around Hilbre until early May and are usually seen with turnstone searching for food on the

Chiffchaff

All three photos courtesy of HiBO

Meadow pipit

seaweed-covered rocks at the north end. At high tide they will roost on the cliff ledges and it is here that the few over-wintering rock pipits may also be seen.

The north end of Hilbre is an excellent place for birdwatching with red-throated diver and great crested grebe being regularly seen. Other less common birds arrive occasionally and these can include great northern and black throated divers along with smaller grebes, pink-footed geese, golden-eye, red-breasted merganser and scaup.

Stonechat

When there is a north-westerly gale, sea watching can produce some really good sightings. Arctic skua can often be seen with the occasional great and long-tailed skuas and pomarine. During October Leach's petrel, guillemot and razorbill may be spotted and in November there is a slight chance of seeing little auk.

Around October, Brent geese begin to arrive back and the count in the winter of 2004/5 was in the region of 55. These flocks can include pale and dark-bellied birds.

Many passerines (perching birds) are migrating at this time of year and goldcrest, chiffchaff and the occasional blackcap have been recorded.

Thrushes and finches pass through and if the weather turns severe lapwings can be seen on their way to Ireland. Snow buntings are also seen in the winter.

Peregrine falcons are often seen around the islands in the winter. They now breed on Wirral.

Arctic tern

Snow bunting

It is in autumn that the numbers of waders begin to build up in the estuary. These include redshank, turnstone, oystercatcher, grey plover, knot, dunlin and curlew. Numbers of these increase to several tens of thousands for the winter and are a fabulous sight when seen swarming in the estuary. They can also be seen from the mainland at West Kirby and Red Rocks on the high tides. It is very important not to disturb the birds, especially for a couple of hours either side of high tide.

Spring and early summer

Spring is another good time for birdwatching on Hilbre with this being the peak migration time for returning summer migrants that have wintered in Africa and are returning to Northern Europe to breed.

White and grey wagtails and meadow pipit begin to appear in late March. The first wheatear, chiffchaff and willow warbler arrive in early April sometimes in very large numbers if the weather conditions are right for the island. (Over 100 willow warblers at one time have been counted.) Ring ouzel can appear in late March and again in early May and are usually seen in the short-cropped grass on the west side of Hilbre or Middle Eye.

Great skua

Sandwich tern

Raptors are seen from Hilbre in the springtime, the most notable one being osprey usually passing through in April and May. Sparrowhawk, marsh harrier, kestrel and even merlin have also been recorded and buzzards are being increasingly seen since the dramatic increase in numbers on Wirral. Long and short-eared owls are occasionally spotted from the islands.

Sea watching can be surprisingly productive in spring. An easterly wind may bring good numbers of little gulls and the first gannets, skuas, little, common, arctic and sandwich terns are often seen in April and May.

Long-eared owl

By the end of April, tree pipit, yellow wagtail, whinchat and Greenland wheatear can be seen whilst redstart, sedge warbler, whitethroat and the odd garden warbler will begin appearing in early May. By late May the number of common migrants will have lessened but spotted flycatcher may still pass through.

Birds in summer

June is often a very quiet month on Hilbre for birds. All the migrants are at their breeding grounds and only the small breeding population of birds are present.

Meadow pipits and skylarks regularly breed on both Middle Eye and Hilbre. They are ground nesting birds and it is especially important not to disturb them at this time.

Hilbre's small population of linnets (between 10 and 20 breeding females) is extremely important, as the linnet is a scarce bird and is on the British Red Data List of declining breeding birds.

Shelduck and mallard successfully breed on the islands and crows may use the chimney of Telegraph house to raise their young.

Peregrine falcon

Occasionally blackbirds and robins breed on Hilbre and wrens are becoming increasingly successful.

Once again sea watching can be very rewarding with counts of the beautiful Manx shearwater reaching several hundred in any one day if the weather conditions are right.

June and July is the best time of year to see storm petrel from Hilbre. They spend much of their lives at sea, breeding on rocky offshore islands around the coast of Britain.

Waders in the estuary

Tern numbers begin to increase in July when several hundred common and sandwich terns and up to 200 little terns may be fishing at high tide off the north end of Hilbre. As the tide drops they can be seen and heard on the sandbanks that surround Hilbre and even on the shore at West Kirby.

Four species of skua, arctic, great, pomarine and sometimes long-tailed can arrive at the same time as the terns. On 7th June 1987 all these four species were recorded – an unusual event!

During the summer months, herons can always be seen fishing around the islands.

Early Autumn

The autumn migration begins in August, bringing back many of the species seen in spring after they have finished breeding further north.

If the weather conditions are right (north-east wind and overcast at dawn) willow warblers will pass through in great numbers. Other migrants at this time of year include wheatear and the occasional whinchat. By the end of August and the start of September, spotted and pied flycatchers, redstart, garden warbler, goldcrest and whitethroat may pass through.

Waders also begin to fly through the area and can include whimbrel, common and curlew sandpipers and little stint. They may be found at the south end of Hilbre in amongst flocks of dunlin and sanderling.

The best conditions for sea watching are when there has been a continuous period of strong north-westerly wind and squalls of rain. This is when storm petrel and Manx shearwater may be seen. From the end of August right through September, Hilbre and North Wirral are two of the best places in Britain to see Leach's petrel.

Roosting turnstones

Nature

Insects

Peacock

Orange tip

The islands are a wonderful place for insects, especially during the late spring and summer. Some live on the islands permanently but there are many that are migrants with red admiral and painted lady butterflies travelling from as far away as southern Europe and North Africa. These arrive in spring and early summer and any seen later on in the year will be their offspring. They cannot usually over-winter successfully in Britain although it appears that red admirals are succeeding in small numbers.

Buff tip moth

Having the ability to fly leads to many insects coming from the mainland, finding the conditions to their liking, and successfully establishing themselves. This has made it a little difficult to

determine which insects are truly native to the islands. Whether native or not, there are many other butterflies that can easily be seen. The common ones include grayling (flying in August), small, green-veined and large white, small tortoiseshell, gatekeeper, and common blue. The common blue will often be seen laying its eggs on birdsfoot trefoil, the larval food plant. Smaller numbers of meadow brown, small copper, peacock, speckled wood and orange tip can also be spotted. The comma

Six spot burnet moths

Grayling

is a very rare visitor but a good place to look for butterflies in the summer is amongst the thistle beds towards the north end of Hilbre.

Although there are many species of butterfly to be found, Hilbre is well known for the number of moths that have been recorded by the members of HiBO and other volunteers. Easily seen are the day-flying moths which include silver Y, 6 spot burnet and cinnabar moth. More conspicuous are the caterpillars of the cinnabar moth feeding and occasionally decimating the poisonous ragwort. These caterpillars are unaffected by the poison but pass it on to potential predators. Careful observation will reveal caterpillars of the buff-tip moth eating the birch leaves in the observatory garden in August. The red and black caterpillars of the garden and ruby tiger moths feed on a variety of short plants, wandering around looking for pupation sites.

Cinnabar moth

Most of the moths that Hilbre is best known for are nocturnal and have been found by the use of a moth trap. These include mallow, netted pug and marbled coronet. The mallow, as the name suggests, feeds on the introduced mallow particularly around the observatory building. Netted pug can sometimes be found resting by day in May or early June on cliff faces, especially near its food plant, the native sea campion. Marbled carpet and campion moths also feed on the sea campion.

Cinnabar moth caterpillars

In recent years the numbers of dragonflies and damselflies have steadily increased. The common darter dragonfly and blue-tailed damselfly are by far the commonest species. Southern hawker dragonfly is regularly seen and emperor and brown hawker dragonflies can be observed laying their eggs in the brackish pond. Other species seen fairly frequently are common and migrant hawker dragonflies and the common blue damselfly.

A bumblebee *Bombus monticola* was present until the 1990s but has not been found recently. This was one of the very few lowland sites in the country for this bumblebee and was considered very special, as it is a moorland specialist.

Southern hawker dragonfly

Common blue damselflies

Comma

Nature

Flowers

Thrift

Thrift

The three Hilbre islands are the main rocky coastal habitat in the area, so many of the plants growing there are of particular interest, with a few being locally rare.

For such a small area there is quite a large diversity of plant species all of which have to tolerate the desiccating action of both salt spray and wind. To do this plants have evolved various ways of conserving water. Thrift for example has needle-like leaves to reduce the risk of the foliage drying out. Sea beet, sea campion and scurvy grass have a thick waxy layer covering the foliage, which seals both leaves and stems, keeping the water in. This makes the leaves appear tough and leathery with shiny foliage. Sea sandwort has fleshy leaves that store water and rock sea-spurrey has very sticky, hairy leaves that prevent desiccation. Many of the plants are perennial and have

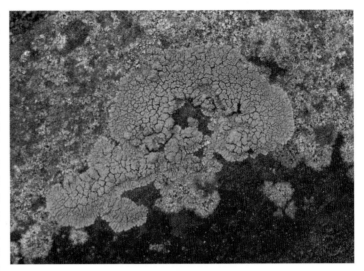

Yellow splash lichen

extensive woody root systems that help anchor them firmly during gales.

There are a few lichens growing on the rocks, mainly on the eastern side of the islands. These include yellow splash lichen *Xanthoria parietina* growing in the splash zone just above high water and sea ivory *Ramalina siliquosa* a tufted lichen that can be found in close proximity to the sea. In stormy seas these tufted lichens can be torn from their sandstone substrate.

Although there are flowers throughout spring, summer and autumn, the best show is in the spring. Spear-leaved orache, Ray's knotgrass, sea sandwort and various grasses such as perennial rye grass, can all be found on Little Eye.

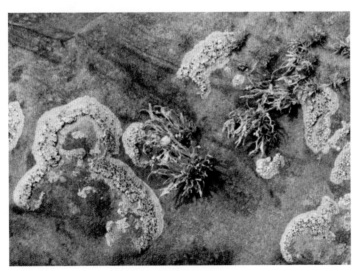

Lichens including sea ivory

Rock sea-spurry

The soil here is predominantly wind blown sand with a very low humus content and yet in summer the pretty sea mayweed comes into flower.

Middle Eye has its fair share of colourful flowers and with this island being one of the main roosting sites for birds, there is a ready supply of natural fertilizer. This enables the growth of some plants, especially sea beet and scurvy grass, to become quite luxuriant.

On both Hilbre and Middle Eye, one of the earliest plants to flower is the Danish scurvy grass, forming a swathe of sweet-scented white flowers. There are also daffodils that make a wonderful splash of early colour. The carpets of bluebells found in May are quite unexpected as bluebells are usually associated with woodland. The delicate flowers of pignut also appear in May and in a good year the pink thrift is spectacular. Yellow birdsfoot trefoil adds to the glorious splash of colour with the white sea campion competing for attention.

However, Hilbre Island itself is where most of the really interesting plants can be found.

Rock sea-lavender *Limonium britannicum ssp celticum* which flowers in July, is one of Hilbre's specialities. This subspecies of rock sea-lavender is only found in five places in the world, all of which are in Britain. It is therefore endemic to the British Isles and is classified as near threatened in the Red Data Book. This pretty little perennial plant has a basal rosette of small leaves from which a branching flowering stem will grow. The lilac/lavender flower clusters each have five petals and the plant can produce up to 500 seeds, which are

Scurvy grass

Birdsfoot trefoil

Rock sea-lavender

distributed by the wind. It has colonised the sandstone crevices on the west side of Hilbre and amongst the western grassy areas is spreading very well. It thrives in the salt spray on the windy side of the island but will not tolerate being trampled on.

Another internationally scarce species present is sea spleenwort *Asplenium marinum* a type of fern found on the cliffs on the east side of Hilbre. This plant can only survive in the presence of sea spray. It has bright green leathery-looking fronds each with a red-brown stalk and a green mid-rib. It produces spores on the underside of the fronds, which ripen in mid-July to mid-August.

Another adaptation by plants to survive on Hilbre's exposed location is small size, so close examination can be rewarding. Easily overlooked when not in flower is sea milkwort. This has tiny pink flowers and grows in the crevices of the sandstone rocks.

Buckshorn plantain

Sea mayweed

Ling (heather)

Sea spleenwort

Sea milkwort

Sea purslane

Sea beet

Rock sea-spurrey is another very pretty plant that is present. It grows on the sea walls, rocks and cliffs and is a small, sticky, prostrate perennial with a woody base. The pink flowers have five petals and are larger and brighter than other related coastal species.

Buckshorn plantain grows all over the islands being another marine specialist. It is a biennial herb and has a flat rosette of leaves looking a little like a branched antler, hence its common name. The yellow-brown flowers are best seen in June.

In August ling and bell heather are in flower together, along with the delicate blue flowers of harebell and sheeps-bit scabious.

A few bushes and trees survive on Hilbre. Blackthorn, elder and sycamore provide food and cover for migrant birds and the Heligoland traps belonging to HiBO have been sited over these bushes. The Duke of Argyll's tea plant was deliberately planted and is now naturalised.

Slender spike rush, another rarity for the area, grows in the brackish marsh that has developed around the pond on Hilbre. Also found here are brookweed, parsley water-dropwort, saltmarsh rush, sea club-rush and common sedge.

Livestock grazing in the past has influenced the type of vegetation present but, as there are now no herd animals, bracken is unfortunately invading parts of the islands. To help control this, volunteers are pulling this bracken out under the direction of the Coastal Ranger and helping to keep it under control. However, no livestock on the islands means that some of the poisonous ragwort can be left as an invaluable food source for many insects, including the cinnabar moth caterpillar.

Sea plantain

Nature
Mammals

Atlantic grey seal

Common seal

Photo courtesy of HiBO

Rabbits lived on the two larger islands for a long time with their numbers fluctuating widely throughout the centuries. Around the turn of the 19th century there were at least 200 rabbits on Hilbre. These were eradicated over a few years by the efforts of local poachers in conjunction with the telegraph keeper of the time. There are records of rabbits in 1939 but in 1955 the population was totally exterminated by myxomatosis and none have been seen breeding on the islands since then.

Now there is only one resident mammal, the short-tailed field vole. These small rodents normally prefer long grass to protect them from their predators but will sometimes be found breeding under the corrugated tin sheets in the

Seals on Hoyle Bank

paddocks on Hilbre. They are prolific breeders and an important source of food for many predators. Kestrels have bred on Hilbre in years when the population of field voles was high.

There are records of some unlikely mammal visitors that have made the journey across the estuary to visit the islands. Occasionally foxes and grey squirrels are seen and if they choose to visit in the spring this can be devastating for the ground nesting birds when the eggs will quickly be found and eaten. Other visitors to the islands are weasels, rats, hedgehogs, mice and bats. In 2002 a stoat was amongst the culprits blamed for completely decimating the eggs of the skylarks that were nesting.

Short-tailed field voles

Photo courtesy of HiBO

Fox footprints on Hilbre

Atlantic grey seals haul out on Hoyle Bank during low tide. They can easily be seen and heard from the islands. The numbers are at their greatest during the summer and the highest count of 579 was recorded in 2000. They return to their breeding grounds for the winter and only a few non-breeding individuals and juveniles remain around the islands at this time. It is uncertain where the seals go to breed but Ramsey Island in Pembrokeshire, the Isle Of Man and parts of Scotland are possible breeding grounds. It is even possible that some breed in Ireland. Common seals are only occasionally seen. The seals become inquisitive in summer and on high tides will come quite close to the islands especially the north end of Hilbre.

In summer it is possible to see harbour porpoise and bottle-nosed dolphin from the north end of Hilbre when the sea is very calm. It will be interesting to see what effect the North Hoyle Bank Wind Farm, erected out to sea in 2003, will have on the visiting sea mammals.

Male Atlantic grey seal

Atlantic grey seals off the north end of Hilbre

Conservation

Restored telegraph station and modern navigation light

Hilbre at high tide

Sand patterns

Throughout the year the Hilbre islands provide a sanctuary for birds, plants and other wildlife. The islands are also a very popular place for many visitors at all states of the tide throughout the year.

Hilbre is a nature reserve so a balance must be maintained to protect the wildlife whilst allowing individuals to visit the islands. Various by-laws are in place to legally protect the Hilbre islands and it is hoped that visitors will appreciate the vulnerability of the islands and observe these by-laws.

All the plants, animals and their habitats in the reserve are legally protected and it is an offence to pick or damage any of the plants or disturb any creature. This includes the environment on the rocky shores and it is important to gently return boulders to their original places after observing the creatures underneath them. Camping is not permitted and fires and barbeques are not allowed on any of the islands. Dogs must be kept on a short lead at all times within the reserve and the breeding and roosting birds must not be disturbed. All litter must be taken home and visitors are asked to keep to the main paths and respect the fenced off and private areas.

To protect the wildlife, the rangers employed by WMBC take advice from English Nature and other conservation bodies to determine the best course of action for the conservation of the islands.

Volunteers from the Friends of Hilbre are raising funds for various large and small-scale projects and increasing awareness of all aspects of the nature reserve. They are restoring buildings as well as helping with the clearance of bracken and other gardening jobs to try and preserve the natural habitat where possible.

In 2003, restoration of the telegraph station was completed and it is now an interpretation centre.

In the past, the Victorians built sandstone walls around Hilbre to halt the erosion of the cliffs. More recently retaining walls have been built to prevent slippage of the soil.

The ruined slipway has been temporarily protected with concrete to prevent further damage until it can be repaired. Once funding has been found, the Buoymaster's house will be converted into a community research and study centre.

North Hoyle Bank Wind Farm

Limpets

Acknowledgements & Websites

The idea for this book came from a chance conversation with a visitor on Hilbre who asked me if there was a picture book of the islands. Research found that an up to date publication was not available and the idea for the book was born.

Many thanks go to the following people who have helped me compile this book on the Hilbre islands:
Dave Cavannagh, the present Ranger on Hilbre for his invaluable help and support.
Sue Craggs for providing most of the information on the history section.
Christine Longworth from Liverpool Museum, also for help with the history section.
Pete Sixsmith for drawing the maps and helping with the geology section.
Diane Bennett formerly of the Wirral Ranger service for help with the rocky shores and estuary section.
Christine Smyth from the Wirral Ranger service also for help with the rocky shores and reading through the text.
Hilary Ash and **Barbara Greenwood** from Wirral Wildlife Trust for their help with the flowers section.
Pete and **Steve Williams** from Hilbre Bird Observatory for permission to use information from their website and annual reports in this book.
Pete Williams also kindly gave me permission to use a few of the photographs taken by HiBO members in this book.
Gavin Broad from HiBO for advice on the section on insects.
Val McFarland for permission to use her photo of the north cone.
Mathilde Baker-Schommer for proof reading the book.

Finally thanks to husband **John** for accompanying me over to the islands throughout the years at some ridiculous times of the day and helping me with my determination to complete this book.

All the photographs in this book were taken by **John** and **Margaret Sixsmith** ARPS AFIAP except were otherwise indicated.

Websites for contacting the following organisations: -

Wirral Metropolitan Borough Council (WMBC)	www.wirral.gov.uk
Hilbre Bird Observatory (HiBO)	www.hilbrebirdobs.co.uk
Friends of Hilbre	www.hilbreisland.org.uk
Webcam	www.wirralcam.com
English Nature	www.english-nature.org.uk
(To be known as Natural England from Autumn 2006)	

Dee Estuary with the Great Orme in the distance

Bibliography & Further Reading

"Hilbre The Cheshire Island" - Its history and natural history edited by J.D. Craggs.
This book, first published in 1982, includes a comprehensive scientific insight into the species that were recorded on Hilbre up to its publication. It makes a very interesting comparison to the numbers and species recorded today by HiBO.

Hilbre Bird Observatory annual reports
Available from the Bird Observatory, this booklet is a list of natural history records with emphasis on all the birds monitored throughout the year.
Their members include many specialists in other natural history fields and they record all species identified throughout the year.

"Hilbre the island in a wilderness" - Birds,wildlife and history
by Valerie Mcfarland, Barry Barnacal and John Craggs.
Published in 1983, another interesting small booklet to compare with today's records.

"The Dee Estuary" - Booklet published by the Dee Estuary Conservation Group 1996.

Trinity House - www.trinityhouse.co.uk
Trinity House is the general lighthouse authority for England, Wales, The Channel Islands and Gibraltar, with responsibility for a range of general aids to navigation.

Marine Biological Association occasional publication no 16 (spring 2004)
Report to English Nature on the Sabellaria alveolata reef survey of Hilbre Island co-edited by Christine Smyth from Wirral Rangers.

"Faster than the Wind"
The history of the Liverpool to Holyhead telegraph by Frank Large published in 1998.

"Reminiscenses of an islander"
Translated from Welsh, a personal account by Lewis Jones, telegraph keeper on Hilbre in the early 1900s. His book 'Atgofion Ynyswr' was privately published in Welsh in Liverpool in 1939.

"West Kirby and Hilbre"
by John Brownbill. Published by Henry Young & Sons, Liverpool in 1928.

Sea mayweed on Little Eye

Fiery sunset over Hilbre